Adelaide

Top 10 Everything;

Places, Attractions, Activities, Cuisine, You Should Experience

WHEREVER

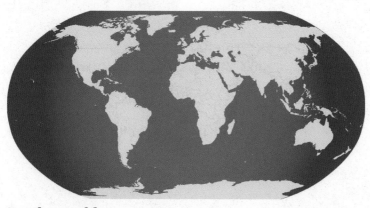

See the world...

Copyright

Table Of Contents

Welcome to Adelaide

Welcome to the enchanting city of Adelaide! Nestled on the southern coast of Australia, Adelaide is a captivating destination that seamlessly combines natural beauty, cultural richness, and a vibrant urban atmosphere. Known as the "City of Churches" and the "Festival City," this cosmopolitan capital of South Australia offers a myriad of experiences for every traveler.

Adelaide boasts a unique charm that sets it apart from other Australian cities. Its well-planned layout, elegant architecture, and abundance of parks and gardens create a picturesque backdrop that entices visitors to explore its wonders. Whether you're strolling along the picturesque River Torrens, discovering hidden laneways dotted with cafes and boutiques, or immersing yourself in the thriving arts and cultural scene, Adelaide has something to captivate every traveler's heart.

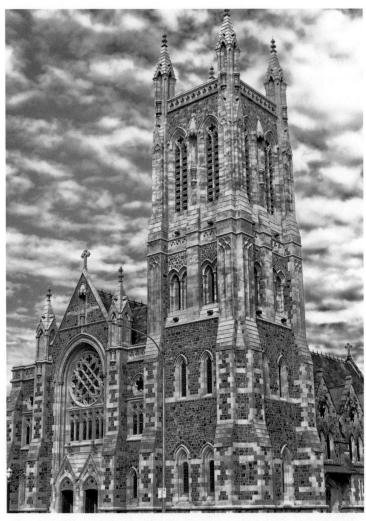

One of the city's defining features is its remarkable food and wine culture. Adelaide and its surrounding regions are home to some of Australia's finest vineyards, producing world-class wines that have earned international acclaim. The city's thriving culinary scene showcases a diverse range of cuisines, from traditional Australian fare to global fusion, all crafted with the freshest local ingredients. Be sure to indulge in a culinary journey through Adelaide's acclaimed restaurants, bustling food markets, and delightful cafes.

Adelaide is also a city steeped in history and culture. The rich heritage of its colonial past is evident in the historic buildings, grand churches, and cultural institutions that grace its streets. The city is home to renowned art galleries, museums, and theaters, offering a wealth of cultural experiences for art enthusiasts and history buffs alike.

For nature lovers, Adelaide is a gateway to breathtaking landscapes and unique wildlife encounters. Just a short drive from the city, you'll find stunning coastal stretches, such as Glenelg Beach, where you can bask in the sun and enjoy the sparkling waters of the Gulf St. Vincent. Further afield, the Adelaide Hills region beckons with its rolling vineyards, charming villages, and picturesque hikes through lush forests.

As you delve into this Adelaide travel guide, you'll discover the best attractions, hidden gems, and insider tips to make the most of your visit. Whether you're seeking a vibrant city experience, a culinary adventure, a cultural immersion, or an exploration of nature's wonders, Adelaide promises to exceed your expectations at every turn. Get ready to be captivated by the warmth of its people, the richness of its history, and the natural beauty that surrounds it. Welcome to Adelaide, a city that invites you to explore, indulge, and create lasting memories.

Top 10 Places to Visit

Adelaide Central Market:

Immerse yourself in a vibrant foodie haven at the Adelaide Central Market, where you can browse through a wide array of fresh produce, gourmet delights, and local specialties. It's a culinary paradise that shouldn't be missed.

Glenelg Beach:

Located just a short tram ride from the city center, Glenelg Beach offers a stunning coastal retreat. Relax on the sandy shores, take a dip in the turquoise waters, or enjoy a stroll along the bustling Jetty Road filled with shops, cafes, and restaurants.

Adelaide Botanic Garden:

Escape to the tranquility of the Adelaide Botanic Garden, a sprawling oasis in the heart of the city. Explore its diverse collection of plants, including the enchanting Bicentennial Conservatory and the iconic Palm House.

Adelaide Oval:

Sports enthusiasts shouldn't miss a visit to the iconic Adelaide Oval. Take a guided tour to learn about the stadium's history and get a behind-the-scenes glimpse of this world-class sporting venue.

Art Gallery of South Australia:

Discover a rich collection of Australian and international art at the Art Gallery of South Australia. From ancient Aboriginal artworks to contemporary masterpieces, the gallery offers a captivating journey through different artistic periods.

Hahndorf:

Just a short drive from Adelaide, you'll find Hahndorf, Australia's oldest surviving German settlement. Explore its charming streets lined with traditional German architecture, indulge in delicious German cuisine, and browse through boutique shops offering unique crafts and souvenirs.

Cleland Wildlife Park:

Get up close and personal with Australia's native wildlife at Cleland Wildlife Park. Walk amongst kangaroos, cuddle a koala, and encounter other iconic animals, making for an unforgettable experience.

Adelaide Hills:

Escape the city and venture into the picturesque Adelaide Hills. Enjoy breathtaking views, visit quaint towns like Stirling and Hahndorf, and explore the region's renowned wineries, offering tastings of world-class wines.

Migration Museum:

Delve into the multicultural history of South Australia at the Migration Museum. Discover stories of migrants and their contributions to the state, providing insights into the diverse cultural fabric of Adelaide.

South Australian Museum:

Uncover the natural and cultural heritage of South Australia at the South Australian Museum. From ancient fossils and artifacts to Aboriginal cultural exhibits, the museum offers a fascinating glimpse into the region's history.

These top 10 places to visit in Adelaide offer a diverse range of experiences, allowing you to immerse yourself in the city's rich culture, natural beauty, and gastronomic delights. Each location is a testament to Adelaide's unique charm and will leave you with unforgettable memories of your visit.

Best Attractions and Activities to enjoy

Barossa Valley Wine Tour:

Embark on a wine-tasting adventure in the world-renowned Barossa Valley, located just outside of Adelaide. Visit the picturesque vineyards, sample exquisite wines, and indulge in gourmet food pairings while taking in the stunning scenery.

Adelaide Zoo:

Explore the Adelaide Zoo, home to over 2,500 animals from around the world. Get up close to beloved creatures like kangaroos, koalas, and pandas, and learn about conservation efforts at this award-winning zoo.

Adelaide Fringe Festival:

If you're visiting during February and March, don't miss the Adelaide Fringe Festival, one of the largest arts festivals in the world. Enjoy an eclectic mix of performances, including comedy shows, live music, theater, and visual arts.

Adelaide Oval RoofClimb:

Take your Adelaide experience to new heights with the Adelaide Oval RoofClimb. Ascend to the roof of this iconic sports stadium and enjoy panoramic views of the city skyline while learning about its history from knowledgeable guides.

Mount Lofty Summit:

Head to Mount Lofty Summit, the highest point in the Adelaide Hills, for breathtaking views of the city, coastline, and surrounding countryside. Hike through scenic trails, enjoy picnics, and capture stunning photographs of the landscape.

Adelaide Festival Centre:

Catch a performance at the Adelaide Festival Centre, a cultural hub showcasing theater, dance, music, and visual arts. Check the program to see what world-class productions are on during your visit.

Adelaide Central Business District (CBD) Walking Tour:

Take a leisurely stroll through Adelaide's CBD to admire its architectural gems, including historic buildings, contemporary designs, and street art. Discover hidden laneways, boutique shops, and charming cafes along the way.

Haigh's Chocolate Factory Tour:

Indulge your sweet tooth with a tour of Haigh's Chocolate Factory. Learn about the chocolate-making process, sample delicious treats, and browse through their delectable range of handcrafted chocolates.

Waterfall Gully:

Escape to Waterfall Gully, a serene natural oasis just a short drive from the city. Embark on a picturesque hike to see the stunning First Falls and immerse yourself in the tranquility of the surrounding bushland.

Adelaide Central Market Cooking Class:

Unleash your inner chef with a cooking class at the Adelaide Central Market. Learn to prepare delicious dishes using fresh, local ingredients under the guidance of experienced chefs, and savor the fruits of your labor afterward.

These attractions and activities offer a diverse range of experiences, allowing you to immerse yourself in

Adelaide's vibrant culture, natural beauty, and culinary delights. Whether you're a nature lover, a food enthusiast, an art aficionado, or simply seeking unique adventures, Adelaide has something to captivate every visitor.

Best Foods and Restaurants

Adelaide is a haven for food lovers, boasting a vibrant culinary scene that showcases a diverse range of flavors and influences. From world-class restaurants to bustling food markets, here are some of the best foods and restaurants to try in Adelaide:

Adelaide Central Market:

Begin your gastronomic journey at the Adelaide Central Market, a bustling food market offering an array of fresh produce, gourmet delights, and multicultural cuisines. Sample delicious cheeses, fresh seafood, artisan bread, and a variety of international dishes.

Africola:

Experience vibrant African flavors at Africola, a popular restaurant known for its bold and creative dishes. Indulge in the grilled meats, flavorful vegetable dishes, and tantalizing spice combinations that make this eatery a must-visit.

Orana:

Immerse yourself in a unique culinary adventure at Orana, a renowned restaurant that celebrates indigenous Australian ingredients and techniques. Enjoy a degustation menu featuring native plants, meats, and seafood, expertly prepared and beautifully presented.

Shōbōsho:

Savor the flavors of Japan and Korea at Shōbōsho, a contemporary East Asian eatery with a focus on charcoal-fired cooking. From yakitori skewers to Korean barbecue and innovative small plates, this restaurant offers a fusion of flavors and a lively atmosphere.

Peel St:

Located in the heart of the city, Peel St is a vibrant eatery serving up modern Australian cuisine with Asian and Middle Eastern influences. The menu changes regularly, offering a creative and exciting dining experience.

Press Food & Wine:

For a sophisticated dining experience, head to Press Food & Wine, a stylish restaurant offering a seasonal menu and an extensive wine list. Indulge in dishes made with locally sourced ingredients and enjoy the elegant ambiance.

Gouger Street:

Known as Adelaide's dining hub, Gouger Street is lined with an array of restaurants serving cuisines from around the world. From Chinese and Vietnamese to Italian and Greek, you'll find a wide variety of flavors to suit every palate.

Chianti:

Experience classic Italian cuisine with a modern twist at Chianti, a long-standing favorite in Adelaide. This elegant restaurant offers a range of traditional Italian dishes made with fresh local ingredients, accompanied by an impressive wine list.

Parwana Afghan Kitchen:

Discover the flavors of Afghanistan at Parwana Afghan Kitchen, a family-owned restaurant that showcases the country's rich culinary heritage. Enjoy delicious kebabs, dumplings, and aromatic rice dishes in a warm and inviting atmosphere.

East End Cellars:

Explore East End Cellars, a wine store and bar located in the trendy East End precinct. Sample a selection of South Australian wines by the glass or purchase a bottle to enjoy alongside a cheese platter or charcuterie board.

These are just a few examples of the exceptional foods and restaurants that Adelaide has to offer. With its diverse culinary landscape and commitment to quality and innovation, the city promises a memorable dining experience for every food enthusiast.

Entertainment and Nightlife

When it comes to entertainment and nightlife, Adelaide offers a vibrant scene that caters to various tastes and preferences. From lively bars and clubs to cultural performances and live music venues, here are some of the top entertainment options to enjoy in Adelaide:

Adelaide Festival Centre: The Adelaide Festival Centre is a cultural hub that hosts a variety of performances, including theater productions, dance shows, musicals, and concerts. Check their program for the latest shows and enjoy an evening of world-class entertainment.

The Garden of Unearthly Delights: During the Adelaide Fringe Festival, The Garden of Unearthly Delights comes to life with a lively atmosphere. This pop-up carnival-like venue features a diverse lineup of comedy shows, live music, circus performances, and interactive experiences.

Adelaide Casino: Test your luck and enjoy a night of entertainment at the Adelaide Casino. Apart from the gaming tables and slot machines, the casino offers bars, restaurants, and live music events, ensuring an exciting evening out.

The Lion Arts Factory: Located in the West End of Adelaide, The Lion Arts Factory is a popular live music venue known for its eclectic lineup of local and international bands and artists. Catch a dynamic performance and immerse yourself in the city's vibrant music scene.

Leigh Street and Peel Street: These atmospheric laneways are home to numerous bars and restaurants, making them perfect for a night out. From hidden speakeasies to trendy cocktail bars and cozy wine bars, you'll find a variety of venues to suit your preferences.

The Producers Bar: Situated on Grenfell Street, The Producers Bar is a popular spot for live music and entertainment. Enjoy a diverse range of performances, including local bands, comedy acts, and themed nights, all while sipping on your favorite drink.

The Elephant British Pub: Step into The Elephant British Pub for a lively night of drinks and entertainment. This iconic pub offers a wide selection of beers on tap, pub grub, and regular live music events that attract a fun-loving crowd.

RCC Fringe: The RCC Fringe is a vibrant pop-up entertainment precinct that comes to life during the Adelaide Fringe Festival. Explore its multiple venues, including live music stages, immersive art installations, and late-night parties, for an unforgettable night of entertainment.

Adelaide Oval Events: Adelaide Oval hosts a range of sporting events, concerts, and festivals throughout the year. Catch a cricket or Australian Rules Football match, or attend a live concert by renowned artists in this iconic venue.

Rooftop Bars: Adelaide boasts a selection of trendy rooftop bars where you can unwind with a drink while enjoying panoramic views of the city. Some popular options include 2KW Bar and Restaurant, Hennessy Rooftop Bar, and The Gallery Rooftop Bar.

From cultural performances to live music venues, energetic bars, and unique entertainment experiences, Adelaide offers a diverse and exciting nightlife scene. Whether you prefer dancing the night away, enjoying live music, or sipping cocktails in a trendy setting, Adelaide has something to cater to every taste.

General Information

Here is some general information about Adelaide regarding language, currency, time zone, entry requirements, local customs, laws and regulations, safety tips, emergency numbers, and medical facilities:

Language:
The official language of Adelaide and Australia is English. However, due to its multicultural population, you may encounter a variety of languages spoken by residents and visitors.

Currency:
The currency used in Adelaide and throughout Australia is the Australian Dollar (AUD). Credit cards are widely accepted, and ATMs are readily available for cash withdrawals.

Time Zone:
Adelaide operates on Australian Central Standard Time (ACST), UTC+9:30, during standard time. However, the state of South Australia does not observe daylight saving time, so it remains at UTC+9:30 year-round.

Entry Requirements:
Most travelers visiting Adelaide will require a valid passport. Visa requirements vary depending on your nationality. It is advisable to check the visa requirements for your specific country before traveling to Australia.

Local Customs:
When visiting Adelaide, it is polite to greet people with a friendly "hello" or "g'day." Australians are generally known for their laid-back and informal nature. Tipping is not as common as in some other countries, but it is appreciated for exceptional service.

Local Laws and Regulations:
It is important to adhere to local laws and regulations while in Adelaide. This includes obeying traffic rules, not smoking in designated areas, and avoiding the use of illegal substances. It is also crucial to respect indigenous cultural sites and sensitive areas.

Safety Tips:
Adelaide is generally a safe city to visit, but it is always advisable to take basic safety precautions. Keep an eye on your belongings, especially in crowded areas. Use reputable transportation

options, particularly during late-night hours. It's also a good idea to be aware of your surroundings and stay in well-lit and populated areas, especially at night.

Emergency Numbers:
In case of emergencies, dial 000 for immediate assistance from police, fire, or ambulance services.

Remember, Australians are generally friendly and approachable, so don't hesitate to ask for help or strike up a conversation if needed.

Please note that this information is provided as a general guide, and it's always recommended to check for the most up-to-date and accurate information regarding entry requirements, local customs, laws, and safety guidelines before traveling to Adelaide or any destination.

Getting Here

Getting to Adelaide is relatively easy thanks to its well-connected transportation system. Here are the common ways to reach Adelaide:

By Air:
Adelaide is served by the Adelaide Airport (ADL), located approximately 6 kilometers west of the city center. It offers domestic and international flights, making it convenient for both domestic and international travelers. Several major airlines operate direct flights to Adelaide from various destinations.

By Train:
The Great Southern Rail operates The Ghan, a renowned train journey that connects Adelaide to Darwin in the Northern Territory. The train provides a scenic and comfortable way to travel, allowing you to enjoy the picturesque landscapes of Australia.

By Bus:
National and regional bus services operate to and from Adelaide, connecting it to other cities and towns within Australia. Companies like Greyhound

Australia and Premier Stateliner offer bus services to and from Adelaide.

By Car:
If you're traveling from within Australia, you can reach Adelaide by car via the national highways. Adelaide is well-connected to major cities like Melbourne, Sydney, and Perth through well-maintained road networks.

By Sea:
Adelaide has a cruise ship terminal, Outer Harbor, which receives various cruise ships during the cruise season. This is an option for those who prefer to arrive by sea.

Local Transportation:
Once you arrive in Adelaide, there are several modes of local transportation available to explore the city and its surroundings. Adelaide has an extensive public transportation system, including buses, trams, and trains, operated by Adelaide Metro. The city center is relatively compact and walkable, making it easy to navigate on foot. Taxis and ride-sharing services like Uber are also available for convenient transportation.

It's always recommended to check for the most up-to-date information regarding transportation options, schedules, and fares when planning your journey to Adelaide.

Accommodation

Adelaide offers a wide range of accommodation options to suit different budgets and preferences. From luxury hotels to budget-friendly hostels and serviced apartments, here are some common types of accommodation you can find in the city:

Hotels: Adelaide has a variety of hotels ranging from luxury 5-star establishments to more affordable options. Many hotels are centrally located, providing convenient access to attractions, dining, and shopping. Some popular areas to find hotels include the Adelaide Central Business District (CBD), North Terrace, and the beachside suburb of Glenelg.

Serviced Apartments: Serviced apartments are a great option for those seeking more space and self-catering facilities. These apartments typically offer a range of amenities, including a kitchenette or full kitchen, living area, and separate bedrooms. They are ideal for families or travelers planning an extended stay.

Bed and Breakfasts: Adelaide has charming bed and breakfast accommodations scattered throughout the city and its surrounding regions.

These establishments often offer cozy rooms, personalized service, and a hearty breakfast to start your day.

Hostels: Budget-conscious travelers can find several hostels in Adelaide that offer affordable dormitory-style rooms or private rooms. Hostels are a popular choice for backpackers, solo travelers, or those looking to socialize and meet fellow travelers.

Holiday Rentals: Adelaide has a selection of holiday rentals available, ranging from apartments to houses and beachside cottages. Websites like Airbnb and Stayz offer a wide range of options for short-term stays, giving you the opportunity to experience a home-away-from-home atmosphere.

Luxury Resorts: For those seeking a luxurious getaway, Adelaide offers a few resorts that provide high-end amenities, stunning views, and top-notch service. Some resorts are located in picturesque settings, such as the Adelaide Hills or along the coastline.

When choosing accommodation in Adelaide, consider factors such as location, proximity to attractions, amenities offered, and your budget. It's advisable to book in advance, especially during peak travel seasons or when major events are taking place in the city.

Note: Due to the dynamic nature of the hospitality industry, it's recommended to check for the latest availability, prices, and policies when making your accommodation arrangements.

Shopping

Shopping in Adelaide is a delightful experience, offering a mix of modern shopping centers, boutique stores, markets, and unique local finds. Here are some popular shopping destinations in Adelaide:

Rundle Mall: Located in the heart of Adelaide, Rundle Mall is a pedestrian-friendly shopping precinct known for its wide range of stores. Here you'll find major retailers, fashion boutiques, department stores, specialty shops, and cafes. It is also home to iconic sculptures, such as the Rundle Mall Balls and the iconic Mall's Balls.

Adelaide Central Market: A must-visit for food lovers and those seeking fresh produce, the Adelaide Central Market is a vibrant and bustling food market. Alongside an array of fresh fruits, vegetables, and gourmet ingredients, you'll find bakeries, delis, and specialty food stores offering a variety of local and international culinary delights.

King William Road: Located in the suburb of Hyde Park, King William Road is known for its boutique shopping experience. The street is lined with fashionable clothing boutiques, home decor stores, beauty salons, and gourmet food outlets. It's a great destination for fashion-forward individuals and those looking for unique gifts.

Burnside Village: Situated in the eastern suburbs of Adelaide, Burnside Village is an upscale shopping center offering a mix of high-end fashion brands, homewares, jewelry, and beauty stores. The outdoor precinct is beautifully designed, providing a sophisticated shopping experience.

Harbour Town Adelaide: Located near the Adelaide Airport, Harbour Town Adelaide is an outlet shopping center where you can find discounted prices on a range of Australian and international brands. It offers a variety of fashion, accessories, and homeware stores, making it a favorite destination for bargain hunters.

Hahndorf: If you're looking for a unique shopping experience, head to Hahndorf, a charming German-influenced town in the Adelaide Hills. Here you'll find boutique shops offering local arts and crafts, jewelry, antiques, and specialty food products. It's a great place to find unique souvenirs and immerse yourself in the town's heritage.

Adelaide Arcade: Dating back to 1885, Adelaide Arcade is a historic shopping arcade featuring a range of specialty stores, fashion boutiques, and cafes. Its beautiful architecture adds to the charm of the shopping experience.

Art and Craft Markets: Adelaide hosts various art and craft markets throughout the year, where you can browse and purchase unique handmade items, artworks, jewelry, and local produce. The Gilles Street Market and Bowerbird Design Market are popular choices for discovering local artisanal products.

These are just a few examples of the shopping experiences Adelaide has to offer. Whether you're searching for fashion, food, art, or unique local finds, you're sure to find something to suit your taste in this vibrant city.

Maps and Transportation

Maps and transportation in Adelaide are designed to make navigating the city and its surroundings convenient and accessible. Here is some information on maps and transportation options in Adelaide:

Maps:

Online Maps: Online mapping services like Google Maps, Apple Maps, and various smartphone apps provide detailed maps of Adelaide. These maps offer directions, public transportation information, and real-time traffic updates.

Paper Maps: You can obtain printed maps from visitor information centers, hotels, or car rental agencies. These maps typically highlight major roads, landmarks, and points of interest in the city.

Transportation Options:

Public Transportation: Adelaide has an efficient public transportation system operated by Adelaide Metro. It includes buses, trams, and trains that provide comprehensive coverage of the city and surrounding areas. You can purchase tickets and travel cards at ticket vending machines or use contactless payment methods.

Trams: The tram network in Adelaide runs along the city's major streets and connects key locations. It provides a convenient way to travel within the city center and popular areas like Glenelg Beach.

Buses: Adelaide's bus network covers a wide range of routes, including both inner-city and suburban areas. Buses are equipped with electronic displays indicating upcoming stops and routes.

Trains: Adelaide's suburban train system connects the city center with outer suburbs and regional areas. Train services are frequent and reliable, offering an efficient mode of transport for both residents and visitors.

Taxis and Ridesharing: Taxis and ridesharing services like Uber are widely available in Adelaide. You can book a taxi through phone services or use ridesharing apps on your smartphone.

Cycling: Adelaide is a bike-friendly city with dedicated bike lanes and paths. You can rent bicycles from various rental shops or make use of the Adelaide Free Bikes scheme, which offers free bike rentals in the city center.

Car Rental: If you prefer to drive, car rental services are available in Adelaide. You can find car rental companies at the Adelaide Airport or in the city center. It's important to familiarize yourself with local traffic rules and parking regulations.

Walking: Adelaide's city center is compact and pedestrian-friendly, making it easy to explore on foot. Many popular attractions, shopping precincts, and dining areas are within walking distance of each other.

It's advisable to plan your transportation options in advance based on your itinerary and destinations of interest. Adelaide's transportation system is well-integrated, allowing for seamless transfers between different modes of transport.

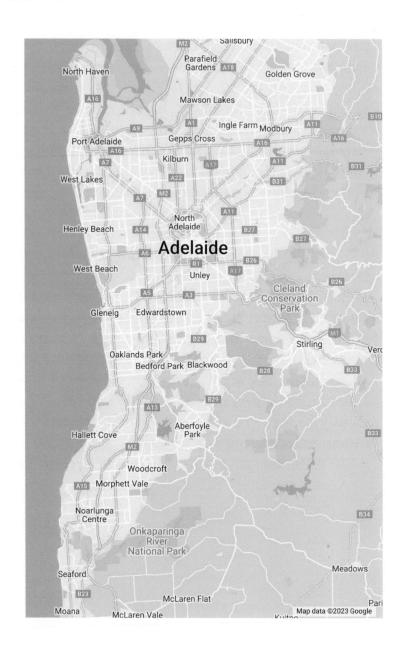

Simple Sample Itineraries

Here are a few simple sample itineraries for Adelaide to help you plan your trip:

Adelaide City Highlights (2 Days)

Day 1:

Morning: Start your day exploring the Adelaide Central Market, where you can enjoy breakfast and browse the wide variety of fresh produce and local delicacies.

Afternoon: Visit the Art Gallery of South Australia and explore the impressive collection of Australian and international artworks. Then, take a stroll along North Terrace, admiring the beautiful architecture and visiting cultural institutions like the South Australian Museum and State Library.

Evening: Head to Rundle Mall for some shopping and dining. Enjoy a meal at one of the many restaurants or cafes in the area.

Day 2:

Morning: Take a tram to Glenelg Beach and spend the morning relaxing by the seaside. Enjoy a swim, take a stroll along the jetty, or grab brunch at one of the beachside cafes.

Afternoon: Visit the Adelaide Botanic Garden, located near the city center. Explore the beautifully landscaped gardens, including the Bicentennial Conservatory and the National Wine Centre.

Evening: Experience the vibrant dining scene of Gouger Street or Peel Street, known for their array of restaurants and bars. Alternatively, catch a show or concert at the Adelaide Festival Centre.

Adelaide Hills and Wine Region (3 Days):

Day 1:

Morning: Drive to Hahndorf, a charming German-inspired town in the Adelaide Hills. Explore the main street lined with boutique shops, art galleries, and cafes. Don't miss the Beerenberg Farm, where you can pick your own strawberries (seasonal).

Afternoon: Visit the wineries in the Adelaide Hills region. Some popular ones include Shaw + Smith, Bird in Hand, and Hahndorf Hill Winery. Enjoy wine tastings and indulge in a leisurely lunch at one of the winery restaurants.

Evening: Return to Adelaide and have dinner at one of the city's acclaimed restaurants.

Day 2:

Morning: Visit Cleland Wildlife Park, located in the Adelaide Hills. Get up close with native Australian wildlife and even have the opportunity to feed kangaroos and hold koalas.

Afternoon: Explore the historic town of Stirling, known for its picturesque gardens and boutique shops. Enjoy a coffee or afternoon tea in one of the charming cafes.

Evening: Take a scenic drive to Mount Lofty Summit and enjoy panoramic views of Adelaide at sunset. Have dinner at the Summit Restaurant, offering fine dining with breathtaking views.

Day 3:

Morning: Drive to the McLaren Vale wine region, known for its world-class wineries. Visit cellar doors such as d'Arenberg, Wirra Wirra, and Coriole Vineyards for wine tastings and enjoy the beautiful vineyard landscapes.

Afternoon: Head to the coastal town of Port Willunga and relax on the stunning beach. If time permits, visit the iconic Port Willunga Jetty ruins.

Evening: Return to Adelaide and enjoy a farewell dinner at one of the city's top restaurants.

These sample itineraries provide a starting point for your trip planning, and you can adjust them based on your preferences and the duration of your stay. Adelaide and its surroundings offer a wide range of attractions and activities to suit different interests, so feel free to customize your itinerary accordingly.

Printed in Great Britain
by Amazon